I0172919

Older Still

Tom Carnicelli

Older Still

Copyright © 2020 by Tom Carnicelli

All rights reserved. No part of this book may be reproduced without the express permission of the author, except in the case of brief excerpts embodied in critical articles and reviews.

Published by Piscataqua Press

An imprint of RiverRun Bookstore, Inc.

32 Daniel Street

Portsmouth, NH 03801

www.riverrunbookstore.com

www.piscataquapress.com

ISBN: 978-1-950381-51-7

Printed in the United States of America

A Note to the Reader

I retired completely in 2013. Like most people, I struggled for quite a while to come to terms with retirement. That struggle is reflected in my first two collections, **Old Guy, Part One (2015)** and **Older Guy (2017),** both published by Piscataqua Press. Now, seven years later, I'm much more comfortable with retirement, and grateful for the opportunities it offers.

Like everyone else's, my life has been affected recently by the coronavirus pandemic, and I've included some poems about the virus in this collection. My main focus, though, remains on my evolving understanding of living in retirement. I've tried to weave the virus poems into the categories of my experience, rather than separating them into a separate section. As in my first two collections, I've tried to avoid writing seriously depressing poems, even when writing about something as grim as the coronavirus. My goal, as ever, is to write about serious topics, but with not too heavy a touch. Readers will decide how well I've succeeded in that effort.

York, Maine, June, 2020

CONTENTS

INTO THE EIGHTIES

TURNING EIGHTY-ONE

I liked turning eighty,
And I enjoyed being eighty.
To me, reaching eighty years old
Was an achievement, a privilege
Not everyone is fortunate to have.
"Wow, I've made it to eighty!"
And eighty is a nice round number.
It has a completeness to it.
It feels like a summing up,
A culmination.

But eighty-one bothers me.
It's the start of a new count,
The first step on the road to ninety,
The road to serious oldness.
And that's a road I'm not (yet)
Eager to take.

Borrowed Time

Since I turned eighty one,
I've started to feel that I'm living
On borrowed time. Sure, we're all
Living on borrowed time, but,
When you get to be my age,
You're facing fact, not possibility.

A month after my birthday,
I rented a fifteen-foot dumpster
And started to clean out the attic
And the cellar, a job I'd always
Planned, but never quite
Got around to doing.

Up in the attic, I crawled
In under the eaves, and dragged
Out stuff I hadn't used for years:
Rugs, suitcases, ski boots.
Then, I hauled it all down
Three flights of stairs.

The cellar had five rooms,
All crammed with useless stuff:
Canning jars with rusted tops,
Wooden storm windows, stacks
Of broken lathes and shingles.
I packed it all in the dumpster.

The attic took about a week.
The cellar took another three.
I worked every day for a month,
From five to eight hours a day,
Using up my borrowed time
Before I get too feeble.

HOSTING

When the table has been cleared
And the dishes washed, when all the guests
Are upstairs in their beds, we sit here,
Thinking back on another pleasant evening,
On all the pleasant evenings we've hosted
In this house. "Well, that was nice,"
One of us will say, and the other will smile
And agree. As we look at each other,
We can feel the familiar question in the air:
"How long can we keep on doing this?"

All summer long, we run a free B and B -
For our relatives and friends. There's always
An extra car parked on our lawn- often,
Three or four. Keeping up this big house,
With its six bedrooms, its wrap-around porches,
Its lawn and five gardens, takes a lot of work;
And, after thirty-five years, we could be
Entitled to a little rest.

We might say we're going to quit, but
We've never seriously considered quitting.
Hosting is what we do in the summer.
We like doing it (most of the time). We like
To see our guests enjoying this house
And coming back year after year.
We can still do this work, and do it well.
Why should we stop?

New Chapter

I'm the oldest one on this bike tour.
That's nothing new, but this time
Things are different. The trails are harder,
Hillier, and sometimes I'm struggling
To keep up. I'm not always in the middle
Of the pack. Today, I rode with the sweeper.
My wife has left me - not for another guy,
But for another bike, one with electric assist.
When we come to the (many) steep hills,
She pushes a button and zips right up,
While I'm down in the granny gears, laboring
Upwards, breathing so hard that the cows
Look up from grazing and stare at me.

You're only as old as you feel,
The saying goes. I must admit I haven't
Been feeling too spry on this trip.
Sure, it's the hardest tour we've taken -
It's labeled "moderate" but there's nothing
Moderate about these monstrous hills.
And yet, the other bikers, women and men,
Seem to be coping well enough.
I'm not exactly decrepit - I did bike
Thirty miles yesterday - but I'm starting
To wonder whether my age is finally
Catching up with me. A sad thought...

But wait! There's another chapter
To this story. I borrowed my wife's bike
Today, and I, too, zipped up the hills.
Best of all, I felt twenty years younger.
Maybe it's time to revise the old saying:
You're only as old as technology
Lets you feel.

DAILY NEWS

Our state has few fatalities,
But the daily list usually includes
" A man in his eighties," and
"A woman in her seventies."
That's us. Those descriptions
Are exactly who we are.

This isn't rare. It happens often,
Maybe three days a week.
We have a hard time responding.
I might say something like
"There we are again."

But that sounds more jaunty
Than I feel. Actually, I
Don't feel much of anything.
They said it would strike
Older people more,

And that's what it's doing -
The experts got it right.
My wife, though, takes our weird
Inclusion in the daily count
More personally; she sees
It as a kind of threat.

Today's report had a twist:
"A man in his seventies" and
"A woman in her eighties." That
Might describe some other couple
(Hundreds, probably) but not us.
We appreciate the day off.

LOSING A YEAR

I have no right to complain.
People are losing their jobs,
Their life's savings, their relatives,
Even their own lives. All
I'm losing is some time.

This virus could last a year,
Maybe more. Nobody wants to lose
A year of living fully, but losing
A whole year is a shock when you get
To be over eighty. All of a sudden,
Your stock of years seems a lot
Smaller than you thought.

I'm not complaining. I have
Absolutely no right to complain.
But I do hope they find a cure
For this damn thing soon.

Spouses

BACK TO NORMAL

When we retired, I expected
A nice, normal, unhurried life.
But there's always some big event
On our calendar: a reunion, a visit,
A holiday, a trip. If we could just
Get past these things, our lives
Would settle down.

And then we could live
The normal life I envisioned.
We'd have time to read books,
To sit and talk to each other,
To have cocktails before dinner
And leisurely meals with music
And candles.

My father, who had Alzheimer's,
Always wanted to go "home."
Poor guy, he never found it,
Even in his own house. I feel
A lot like he did. I keep waiting
For things to return to "normal,"
And they never do.

NORMAL

He sounds like an old fogey
Sometimes, but he's really not.
When our life gets really hectic,
We both can feel overwhelmed.
But neither of us would prefer
To sit inside by ourselves,
Doing nothing special.

Actually, sitting inside
Drives him nuts. He pesters
Me to go out - for breakfast,
Lunch, dinner, or just for coffee;
And, yes, we do have meals
With candles and music, but
Usually in restaurants.

He always complains
Before going to big events,
Or taking trips, or entertaining
Guests , but he always enjoys
Himself. And If there's nothing
Special to look forward to,
He starts to grumble.

I like the busy life
We have now. It keeps us
Engaged in the world, more so
Than when we were working.
It's our new "normal," and it's
Better than sitting at home.
He knows that, too, even
If he won't admit it.

LAUNDRY

I refuse to have my wife do my laundry.
She would do it, cheerfully, and do it
Far better than I can, but why should she
Have to deal with my grungy underwear?
When I was a boy, my mother did my laundry,
But I'm an adult now. Shouldn't an adult
    Clean up his own messes?

My wife never expects me to do her laundry,
And she prefers that I leave her wet clothes
In the washer if I happen to find them there.
(I'm hard on delicates.) She respects my desire
To iron, but, sometimes, when we're going
Somewhere special, I find hanging in my closet
    A freshly ironed shirt.

FUZZIES

What are they, those balls
Of dust that appear on our floors?
My wife calls them dust bunnies.
I call them dust kitties, or just kitties.
We both agree that they're small
And fuzzy, which could apply
To bunnies or to kitties.
She argues that they multiply rapidly,
Like bunnies, and she has a point.
But I argue that they curl up in balls,
Like kitties, and that they don't
Have pointed ears. She argues
That bunnies can tuck in their ears
And curl up, too.

The internet won't help us.
It lists both names and others, too.
We've both been accosting
Strangers, and more of them,
It seems, agree with her.
I guess I lose, and so I get
To vacuum up our little friends.
Let's see, where can they be?
"Here, kitty, kitty."

14

CLOSE CALLS

As we get older, our wives
Watch us like hawks, afraid we'll do
Something risky and dangerous,
Something stupid, they say.
But we are guys, after all,
And even the most cautious of us
Do take risks on occasion. We all
Have lists of close calls in our minds.

Once, I was skating on black ice
So thin I could see fish swimming
Beneath it. And I used to believe
That, if you're skating fast enough,
You keep on going forward
If the ice breaks beneath you
(You don't; you go straight down).

Like all of us, I've got stories
Involving chain saws, ladders,
And trees. Over the years, I've had
To swing from a tree or two.
Just last year, I was up on a ladder
When my chain saw got stuck
In the limb I was trying to cut.
There I was, twenty-five feet up,
With the damn saw wedged in the tree.
When I got out of that one, I told
My wife about it. She thought
It was stupid. And, of course,
She was right: it was stupid.
But it was fun.

SOCIAL DISTANCING

I don't do social distancing well.
When I meet somebody I know,
I tend to move closer to them
As we talk. It's not something
I notice, but my wife does.

After the conversation is over,
She scolds me. She tells me
I was much closer than six feet,
While I thought I'd maintained
A perfectly safe distance.

If this continues (and I think
It will), I'd be perfectly willing
To wear a leash. Then, she could
Hold me back, and I could
Strain forward, yapping.

SPOUSAL DISTANCING

What if the governor mandated
Spousal distancing? How would we comply?
Well, we'd be O.K. with sleeping: one of us
Could stay in our double bed; the other
Could sleep on the couch downstairs.
Eating separately would be easy enough:
One could eat at the table; the other,
At the kitchen counter. Riding in the car
Would be difficult. There are less
Than six feet between the driver's seat
And the back seat on the right;
So, the passenger would have to lie
On the floor behind the back seat
(Not so good, but we only take
Short trips now). The biggest problem
Would be the lack of touching -
Kissing, hugging, that sort of thing.
I guess we could blow kisses
From across the room.

But we would never agree to do
These things. We want to keep
Doing everything together, just as
We do now. We'd defy the order.
We'd rebel. We'd turn on *Les Mis*
At top volume and march...

But no governor would ever give
Such an order. When people are stuck
Inside with not enough to do, these are
The kinds of things they dream up.

FINISHING TOUCH

My wife is refusing to cut my hair.
She says she likes it long -
And that may be true - but the real reason
Is that she's afraid to do it.
I can sympathize. If she asked me
To cut her hair (which she never would),
I'd be petrified.

Sooner or later, I'll have to force
The issue. I'll get some scissors,
Hack away on one side, and show her
How It looks. Then, she'll take over
And finish the job. And you know what?
If she does this job the way
She does everything else, my hair
Will look pretty darn good.

ADULTS & CHILDREN

PARENTHOOD

Parenthood, they say, is a job
That never ends. And they're right,
Up to a point. But the point does come.
When all the drama and the trauma -
The schools, the weddings, (the divorces),
The births, the jobs, the houses -
Are over, and your children
Seem relatively settled, a lull sets in.

You feel free to travel, to stay away
As long as you like, to spend
As much money as you like.
You leave them your itinerary, with dates
And places and numbers, but you know
Your children won't use it.
They won't even think about you
While you're gone, and you,
For a while, won't think about them.

CATCHING UP

"You'll never catch up to me,"
I joked to my former student.
I was talking about years.
She was nineteen years old
When we first met, and I was
Forty-six. That's a huge gap.

We've kept in contact
For over thirty-five years now.
I've been to her wedding,
And to her daughter's,
To her college graduation,
And to her daughter's.
I've watched her guide
Her two children into adulthood,
And watched her establish
A strong marriage and a long,
Successful career.

Those are the same things
I myself have done. And now
That I'm retired and more or less
Standing still, how, exactly,
Are the two of us so different?
Maybe my joke was all wrong.
What more would she have to do
To catch up to me?
Maybe she already has.

This Year

Three years ago, we were not sorry
To see this little girl taken up to bed.

This year, we can't get enough of her.
She's so lively, so funny, so smart.
She seems far more interesting
Than any conversation we adults
Might start. Why the big difference?

She's gotten older. Could we
Have gotten wiser?

In the Pews

Look at that poor little boy
In the front pew. He squirms
And he wiggles and he fidgets.
He flops into his grandpa's arms
And lies there limp for a minute;
Then, he's moving again, crawling
Right under the seat.

Church can be boring
If you don't know what's going on.
(It can also be boring if you do.)
Most of us can sit there, silent
And still, but most kids
Can't do that. And some old guys
Either can't or won't.

During one long sermon,
An old guy in front of us said,
In a spectacular stage whisper,
"When will this old windbag
Be done?" His wife no doubt
Was mortified, but some of us
Wanted to applaud.

A Salute to Seniors, 2020

You walk through the halls like a king
Surveying his domain. Mr. Kelly,
The Math teacher who used to terrify you,
Is now your friend. "Hi, Jim," he says
As you walk by. All the teachers
Are like that now. They're proud of you.
There's no more "us" and "them;"
There's just one school, one town.

The younger kids pay you homage.
You joke around with your buddies,
But you notice that some of them
Aren't ready to move on. And some
Of the kids you used to look down on -
The ones not in your circle- are now
More interesting than you thought.

At the baseball game after school,
You start at shortstop. You've waited
Three years for the chance to start,
And now you have the skills to do it.
For the first time in a long while,
The team is doing well, and dozens
Of townspeople come to watch.

In May, you go to the prom,
With the girl who's been your friend
And girlfriend for two years now.
She looks fantastic, and you look like
You really belong in that stylish tux.

In the final week, you do what
You've aimed at for years, march
In your cap and gown; and, again,
The town is there to cheer you on.

None of these things will ever happen.
You won't get to do any of them.
In the midst of all the sickness and death,
Your losses might seem trivial.
They're not; you've lost a special time,
A time we had, a time you should have had.
But your elders cannot change the world
For you. We can only tell you
"We sympathize. We understand."

Beginnings

The Garment Worker*

A middle-aged man,
Seated at a work bench,
His fingers guiding cloth
Through a sewing machine,
All his attention focused
On the task at hand.

He's Jewish, of course.
We know from his yamulke,
And from this place, where
Jews were in charge, and
Where many an immigrant
Got a start.

Including my grandfather,
Who came over from Italy
At age fifteen. The Jews
Taught him the garment trade.
They also taught him English
(Such an accent!)

This bronze figure
Is a tribute to all those
Immigrants who helped
To build this country. It's also
A message for the future:
This, my friends, is how
Serious work is done.

* An eight-foot high bronze statue called "The Garment Worker" is permanently located in the heart of the New York City Garment District, at 555 Seventh Ave., between 39th. and 40th. streets. The statue was created by an Israeli - American sculptor, Judith Weller.

FAMILY HEIRLOOM

It's a potato masher
With a three-looped metal head
And a wooden handle painted
An unusual pea-green.
Since it's the only thing left
From my grandparents' household,
We call it the family heirloom.
It's hardly a great treasure, but
We'd treasure any keepsake
From the two of them.

They probably got it in 1907,
When they married in New York City.
He'd come over from Italy, alone,
At age 15; she was already here.
They went on to do very well:
He, as a designer of women's clothes;
She, as the classic Italian mother.
They had four children, two boys,
Too girls, and bought a big house
In the Boston area.

And their children, of course,
Good Italian kids, settled there, too.
Those were the days when children
Were expected to visit their parents
For Sunday dinner; and, every Sunday,
My father, my mother, and I
Would climb into our DeSoto and drive
An hour to my grandparents' house.
My uncle and aunts and their families
Would all be there, too.

There'd be a dozen or more of us,
And we sat at the table all afternoon.
I remember the endless parade of food
My grandmother prepared - the soup,
The spaghetti, the roast, the dessert.
(I could have stopped with the spaghetti).
But what I remember best is my two
Grandparents, the king and queen,
Sitting at the ends of the table,
Happy and proud.

We had used my grandmother's
Green masher for years when we visited
The Tenement Museum in New York City.
And there, in the model kitchen
Of an immigrant family in the year 1910,
That special pea- green was everywhere -
On tables and chairs, even on walls.
And, right on the kitchen counter
Was a pea- green potato masher,
Identical to ours.

And so our humble masher
Is not just a family heirloom;
It's a piece of American History.
But we're not about to sell it,
Or give it to some institution.
We're going to keep it right here
In our kitchen and use it.
If you really want to see one,
Just go to the Tenement Museum.
They have one just like ours.

No More Tales

Our niece, newly married,
Needed a bed for her guest room,
And we had a twin bed up in our attic.
We offered it to her, and she accepted,
Sight unseen - a good thing, since
The bed needed some work.
I got rid of the scratches,
Bought back its deep mahogany luster,
And, when we took it to our niece,
She was thrilled to have it.

And we were thrilled to see it
Used again. It had a long history.
It was a wedding gift, one of a pair
Of twin beds my father's parents
Gave to my father and mother.
That was back in 1936, when couples
Still used to sleep in twin beds.
During their lifetimes, my parents lived
In three houses, and I can still remember
Those two beds, set side by side,
In the bedrooms of those houses,
Hers always closer to the window,
His closer to the door (and bathroom?).
When my father died, we kept
Only my mother's bed, and moved it
To the center of the room.
She slept in it for ten more years,
And, when she died (at 104),

Her bed was retired to our attic.
But not for long, for now
It 's been given to another pair
Of newly weds, 82 years later.

It's a good story, and
We passed it on to our niece,
But she can't be expected
To remember stories
About people she never knew.
In time, nobody will remember
Whose bed this was or where
They got it. Only the bed itself
Will remain, and it will tell
No more tales.

Right Down the Aisle

I'm not one of those old guys
Who totters around, pushing the shopping cart
Behind his wife, but, on this day,
I 'd offered to help.

I was hunting for Ritz crackers
And came upon a row of little red boxes
With pictures of wild animals
On them: animal crackers!

I used to love animal crackers
(Though I still believe they're cookies,
Not crackers) and I was pleased
To find they're still around.

They got me thinking
About some of my other old favorites.
Does Hood still make Hoodsies?
I'm pretty sure they do.

I used to love Hoodsies,
For the ice cream and the pictures on the back
Of the lid. I still buy Hood milk today,
Out of loyalty.

And what about Cracker Jacks -
That caramel popcorn and those red peanuts?
I loved to eat them and fish inside
The box for the prize.

Can you still buy Cracker Jacks?
And what about Necco wafers, which I loved
(Except for the licorice ones), and Skybars,
With the four great fillings?

And what's happened to Devil Dogs,
Which I loved before I knew of Whoopie Pies?
Does anybody still make these things?
I was pondering these questions

When my wife appeared,
With a very full cart. She'd been looking
For me. "I'm getting Ritz crackers.
They're right down this aisle."

The Hall Light

When I leave the old house
For the winter, I always leave
The hall light on. That light suggests
The house might not be empty.

When I drive by and see that light,
I like to imagine my daughter,
Playing records in her messy room;
My son, working on his coin collection;
Their mother, sitting on the bed,
Reading a magazine.

My children are in their fifties,
And their mother has passed away.
Still, that shining light reveals a truth:
A human house once lived in
Can never be empty again.

CLOTHES

DRESSING FOR WORK

Everybody in my generation has
A story about their old Italian gardener,
A man who wore formal clothes
While working in the family garden.

Ours was named Patsy. He showed up
Every spring, and spent a full week
Getting our garden plot ready, using
Only an old-fashioned shovel.

As a boy, I used to watch him work.
He dug steadily, all day long, but what
I remember best is what he wore:
A suit jacket, a white shirt, and a tie.

After he'd spent the day digging
In the hot sun, that white shirt of his
Would look pretty bad - he'd show up
The next morning in a fresh one.

As a boy, I thought dressing up
To go dig dirt was foolish. My father said
All the old Italian men dressed up for work,
Even the garbage collectors.

I understood them better when I went
To work myself. I wore a coat and tie at work
Almost every day of my life. I chose to do it.
Most of my colleagues chose not to.

I worked at a desk for over fifty years.
I didn't sweat or dig dirt, but I still worked
Pretty damn hard. I was a lot like old Patsy,
But a whole lot easier on white shirts.

CLOTHES AND THE MAN

My plan for retirement
Was to live a life of casual elegance,
To dress in that slightly tattered way
That well-to-do old preppies have:
With a thirty-year-old tweed jacket,
A blue-striped button-down shirt,
Chino pants, cordovan loafers,
And a navy blue cashmere sweater
With a hole in one elbow.

I wear all these things, and I bought
Them at Brooks Brothers, where
All the old preppies shop. Hell,
I'm an old preppy myself (PA'54).
Why, then, don't I look more
Like George Bush, senior, and less
Like an old Italian gardener
In dress-up clothes?

TIGHTY WHITEYS

Like all little boys, I wore
Tighty Whiteys as my underwear -
Jockeys or the more exotic
Fruit of the Loom. They did the job
Just fine. In my early twenties,
Looking for something more adult,
I started wearing boxer shorts.
These were nothing special,
Certainly not uplifting. Still, I fit in
Well In the men's locker room.

Then, somebody (Calvin Klein?)
Changed the world of men's shorts.
They made shorts tight-fitting,
Bold, and sexy. Shorts came in packs
With Adonis-like figures on the cover,
Men with tight, rippling stomachs.
These new shorts came in bright colors,
In red, blue, or yellow; they came
In multi-colors, in tiger stripes.
My wife, tired of seeing me
In sawed-off pyjama bottoms,
Brought some home, and I was
Happy to try them. They felt good
And they looked good, too.
I was hardly the next Adonis,
But they made me feel younger,
Or at least a little less drab.

There was only one problem:
Some of them had no fly-hole.
For an older guy, that's not good.
Adonis may have time to fish around,
But, for us, time is of the essence.
And so, reluctantly, I've come back,
Back to good old Tighty Whiteys,
Which a guy can depend on
In the pinch.

POSSESSIONS

TACKS

If you grew up in New England
When I did, and if you loved skating
And hockey as I did, then Canada
Was a magical place.

It was where Les Canadiens
Came from, intense, dark-browed,
Lightning-fast hockey players
Like Maurice Richard.

And it was where Tacks
Came from, Tackaberry skates,
The finest hockey skates
The world has ever seen.

They were made by CCM,
Canadian Cycle and Motor Company,
And they were made of leather
(Not plastic) and steel.

Tacks were beyond me, I thought,
But, when I finally wore out my old skates,
I found a pair of Tacks on line,
Used but just my size.

They're beautiful to look at,
With boots made of soft, firm leather,
And effortless to skate in. I've
Never skated so well.

Still, I'll never feel
These wonderful skates belong to me.
I'm no Maurice Richard.
I'm not even Canadian.

HANGING THE PAINTINGS

Every year, we rehang the paintings.
We move them around, debating
An inch or two to the right or left.
We love all of them. We remember when
And where we bought them,
How excited we were to find them.
We're still excited to see them
In new positions, new combinations.

These are paintings by unknowns,
Bought at local galleries and shows.
They certainly weren't expensive -
Several cost less than $100. We bought
The gray collage for only $150
(The artist said his rent was due).
The value of these paintings will not
Increase with time- don't expect
To see them on Antiques Roadshow.
They'll never be worth more than
They are to us right now.

NAMES WE CALL THINGS

They start off as specific things -
A vase with a floral pattern, an end table
With a leather top, a painting of a grey cat.
When we stop finding them interesting,
We think of them as "stuff," which
We tuck away in the attic
And forget about.

"Stuff" accumulates. The attic,
And then the spare rooms, become
Cluttered with it. When we can no longer
Avoid noticing it, we make judgments:
Some of it might have value
Someday; the rest of it
We call "junk."

The clutter gets worse,
And we try to get rid of the "junk."
We hold a yard sale on the front lawn
And drag ugly, bulky furniture down
From the attic. At the end
Of the day, the furniture
Is still sitting there.

We drag it to the curb
With a "Free" sign on it, and,
When it's still there the next morning,
We run out of all patience.

"Let's get rid of this shit,"
We cry, as we haul it
Off to the dump.

Some things will never
Become "stuff." Others will go from "stuff"
To "junk," and then to "shit.' Acquire with care.
That cute little tchotchke you're fondling
Will not hold your interest for long.
You'll be calling it "a piece of shit"
Within a week.

SPORTS

BAD LIE

We're walking on the cart paths
In the golf course, one of the few places
That haven't been closed to the public
(Probably because it's private land.)
To discourage people from congregating,
The selectmen have closed most of the places
Where we've been walking - the beaches,
The parks, even the path around the harbor.
I've got to admit that this golf course really is
A beautiful place. This hole has fine, stately trees,
Which I've never noticed before. It's hard
To admire them when your drive lands
Somewhere in the middle of them.
"Well, it's still great to be out here,"
We golfers say, as we get a second ball
Out of the bag. Sure it is.

SPRING SKIING

It's April now, and the snow
Is almost gone, except for the ugly
Black and white piles where the plows
Have dumped it. The lawns are bare
And starting to look green.
Outside the hardware stores,
They've taken away the snowblowers
And put the new lawnmowers
On display. In a week or so,
All the golf courses will be open.
One or two are open already,
With temporary greens.

I'll get the clubs out soon enough,
But I'm not ready to give up skiing.
The trails in the woods still have
Snow. There are gaps, of course -
Patches of mud or standing water -
But I can work my skis around those;
And, on the stretches of bare ground,
I just take off my skis and walk.
It's early April, but I can still get in
Two hours of decent skiing.

One year, on Opening Day,
I skied in the afternoon, then went
To the ballpark still in my ski clothes.
That was on April 10. This year,
I hope to ski even later than that.

MIND GAME

My tennis game is way off.
I used to rely on speed. I'd stand
On the back line and sprint after the ball.
I usually got to it, even those
Mean-spirited drop shots.

This strategy (such as it was)
Is not working so well this year.
I seem to have lost a step (or two).
Shots I'd return with ease
I'm just not getting to.

You can't order a new pair
Of legs from the Internet;
Even Amazon has limits. You have
To rely on the body you have,
And on your mind.

My body still works
Pretty well, but it can't do
The whole thing on its own any more.
I need my lazy, by-stander mind
To kick in and contribute.

RETIREMENT

TWO WAYS

Retired guys go two ways.
Some have something they have
To do every day of the week.
They volunteer, they mentor,
They run for local office, serve
On committees and boards.
These guys have appointments
And meetings all week long.
Their lives are mapped out
On their cell phones.

Other retired guys avoid
Commitments like the plague.
They don't have a schedule.
They have plenty of things to do
But no set times to do them
(Except, of course, for Trash Day).
If somebody needs their help,
They'll volunteer, but they'd
Rather help for five straight days
Than every Tuesday morning.

Neither way is better or worse,
More selfish or more virtuous.
These are free choices people make.
If the first guy feels too busy
(And he will), and the second guy
Feels at loose ends (and he will),
it's nobody's fault but their own.

TRASH DAY

After you retire, you can always
Recognize Saturday and Sunday,
But you lose track of the weekdays.
When you have nothing you have to do,
The days can run together.

Every morning, at breakfast, one of us
Will ask "What day is it?" and none of us
Is really sure. We could, of course, pick up
The newspaper, but that would be cheating.
We'd rather use our own system.

Our trash pick-up day is Wednesday.
That's the one day we have to remember,
And we use it as a guide to the rest
Of the week. Thursday is the easiest;
It's the Day After Trash Day.

Friday is a little harder, as our memories
Start to get hazy. We always agree
(Sooner or later) that we must have
Put out the trash two days ago.
Two Days after Trash Day is Friday.

On Mondays, we use a different strategy.
The Day before the Day Before Trash Day
Is not going to work. We still remember,
Though, that yesterday was Sunday,
And the Day after Sunday is Monday.

Tuesday Is probably the hardest. Sunday
Has gotten hazy in our minds, but, just
In time, Trash Day has popped back in.
We know it's the Day before Trash Day,
And that makes it Tuesday.

Our system was working well
Until a new guy joined us. He kept
Getting us confused; then, we
Finally figured out the problem:
His trash day is Thursday.

SEVEN YEARS LATER

We'd just returned from a cruise,
Two weeks along the coast of Norway
(In the middle of January, no less!)
And our children had come up to hear
About it. It was a great trip.
We showed them our pictures and told
Our stories. They were happy for us.

Then, we asked about their lives.
Our two children and their spouses
Are all in their fifties, their prime years.
They seem so busy! They like their work,
And believe, strongly, In its importance,
But working seems to be
Almost all they do.

As we talked, the contrast
Between our lives was striking.
They talked of the daily pressures
And challenges they deal with; we
Talked of our latest adventures.
They were the working people;
We were the gay retirees.

Our life seemed almost frivolous
In comparison to theirs. Working,
Of course, is more important;
The whole world depends upon it.
But what we do In retirement
Has value, too; it's much more
Than fun and games.

On our cruise, we enjoyed
The restaurants, the musical shows,
The afternoon high tea. We also
Stood in the dark for three hours
To watch the Northern Lights; we
Lived in the Polar Night; we touched
The markings on a reindeer's ear.

When I was working, I used
To leave home just before sunrise.
We live right by the ocean, and
The sky at that moment is amazing:
Bright orange rising from the horizon,
Banks of purple clouds. I always wished
I could sit for a while and look at it.
Now that I'm retired, I do.

UNSUNG HEROES

Old Pro

She must be in her sixties now.
She's been waiting in this restaurant
For as long as we've been coming here -
Twenty-five years, at least.
She's a real pro. She never needs
To write our orders down.
Just when we realize we want
More coffee, she brings it over.
She's pleasant but never chatty.
We know her name only because
It's printed on the bill.
We never call her by it.
She's a short, thin woman,
Stronger than she looks.
She handles the heavy trays
By tilting her torso back a little,
And, when her hand begins to shake
While she's pouring our coffee,
She uses her other hand to steady it.

BELLY DANCER ON THE TRAIN

We're on the train back from Boston,
And there's a belly dancer in the seat
Across from us. I know this because
She's talking excitedly on her cell phone,
Describing her night's performance;
Also because she's wearing a costume
With sequins from neck to knee.
She's in her forties, I'd guess, and
She does not have a dancer's body,
Unless, in belly dancing, extra pounds
Are a good thing: the more belly
You have, the more impressive
Your shaking? Maybe that's the rule,
And maybe this excited lady
Is a successful dancer after all.
As she tells her story, it's clear
How seriously she takes her craft,
How much she loves it. Tonight,
She feels, her performance was
A great success. I hope it was.

OLD BAGGER

When you're paying at the register,
You expect to see a kid bagging
Your groceries, not an old guy
With a beard. But there he was -
A real old Mainer, with a long white beard,
A cap with a visor, and a plaid flannel shirt
Beneath his red company apron.
The deep wrinkles in his face
Made him look at least seventy-five.
He looked fit enough, though.
He was thin, stood up straight,
And bagged my groceries quickly.
He was cheerful when I thanked him.

Why was he there?
Was he so poor that he had to take
Any job to get by?
Was there some terrible health crisis
In his family?
Was he just tired of sitting in the house
All winter?

I'll never know, and it's none
Of my damn business, anyway.

WALKING LADY

I call her Walking Lady.
All summer long, I see her
Walking around town.
Among the tourists
In their t-shirts and flip-flops,
She's not hard to find.
She's always all dressed up,
In tailored suits or dresses,
And stylish leather shoes.
She carries a leather bag,
And she always wears a hat,
A firm, wide-brimmed hat.
This lady belongs on Fifth Avenue,
Not in this little seaside town,
But she's here every day, walking:
On the sidewalk by the beach,
On the path along the harbor,
Or right in the village square.

I can't help wondering
Who she is . Mrs. Walker,
Maybe? (Probably not.)
And I wonder where she goes
When the weather turns cold.
Perhaps she walks south
For the winter.

THE GOOD SAMARITAN

We still know their names,
The old gods and heroes: Atlas, Achilles,
King Arthur, Paul Bunyan, Hercules.
Maybe their deeds have been forgotten,
Maybe their names are all we know,
But their fame survives.

But what of the Good Samaritan?
We all remember what he did, but
His name is not recorded.
Would the memory of his deeds satisfy him?
Or is he up there somewhere,
Feeling somewhat miffed?

ROUTINES

SHOWING UP

I go to this mass every Sunday.
It's early, 7:30 in the morning, but
It's no great sacrifice for me to get here.
After all, by six a.m. on weekdays,
I'm at the gym.

I like being here. I see
The same people, in the same seats.
And I, too, sit in the same seat, halfway down
On the left, where I can catch the sun
Through the stained glass.

I try to pay close attention
To the service. I enjoy the familiar
Words and hymns and patterns, and, sometimes,
if I listen closely to a reading or sermon,
I'll get some new understanding.

There are days, though,
When I'm distracted. I just can't respond.
I sit here looking pious, but my mind is elsewhere.
I'm like a non-believer, with ears
That do not hear.

But I am a believer - that, I know.
And I can take comfort from Woody Allen,
Who said that "Showing up is 80% of success."
I may not be a model of devotion
But I do show up.

SIGNS OF SPRING

It's spring. Betsy in her blue hat
Is walking again in the square.

The first signs are back
In April: no ice on the windshield
In the morning, and a slight trace
Of green in the brown grass.

Then come the "April showers:"
Steady rain, day after dreary day,
Leaving the forecasters on t.v.
With nothing good to say.

The grass, of course, does well,
Growing at least an inch or two
A day. All of us call to be sure
We're on our mower's list.

The "May flowers" are mostly
Dandelions, which blossom for a day,
Then leave their long, unsightly stalks
All over our shaggy lawns.

Missing from all of this
Is the sun, which seems to be
On vacation for the month of April
Right through to Memorial Day.

In June, it starts to appear,
And Betsy in her powder-blue sun hat
Starts her daily walking. And that's how
We know it's finally spring.

Old Guy at the Gym

"I'm only eighty-one.'
I wondered if I'd ever say that,
Ever think it. Eighty-one
Seems so damned old, but
Sam, an old guy at our gym,
Changed my mind.

He starts off on the treadmill,
Pounding it , running so hard
You can't help hearing him.
Then, he tours the weight machines,
Pulling or lifting at each one.
He ends each session with his leg-lifts,
Which I always try to watch.
Before he starts, he fastens
A five-pound weight around each ankle.
Then, he lies on the bench
And lifts both legs upward, until
His feet are directly above his head.
He holds his legs straight up
For a while, then brings
Them slowly down.
He does ten lifts a day,
Way more than I could do,
Even without the weights.

Our gym is funny. We're all
Friends, but we don't know
Each other's last names.

Further information seeps out
Slowly. I still don't know
Sam's last name, but, last week,
I found out how old he is.
Sam is eighty-nine,
Going on ninety.

DO IT YOURSELF

You can hire a company.
Two guys will blow the leaves
Into piles, and a truck with a vacuum
Will suck them all up. The whole thing
Will take around two hours, and cost you
Around two hundred bucks.

Or you can do it yourself.
You can rake the leaves into piles,
Pack them by hand into leaf bags,
Load the bags Into your station wagon,
Then drive ten miles to the town dump.
It used to take me a dozen dump runs
(Thirteen bags per run). Add in
The time for raking and loading,
And the whole job always took me
Three or four full days.

Why in the world did I choose
To do this miserable, tedious job,
And for more than thirty years?
It was a matter of principle:
Why pay money when you can
Do it yourself?

Maybe this year
I'll pay the money.
Maybe I won't.

DRY YOUR HANDS

"The Best Way to Dry Your Hands."
I was surprised , and a little amused,
To find an article with that title printed
In the Wall Street Journal. The topic
Seemed a little basic for a sophisticated
Audience. I read the article anyway.

Here's what it said. Dampness is bad.
If you don't dry your hands completely,
They can still have germs. Soggy cloth towels
Are very bad; so are those cloth towels
On rollers. Hot-air blowers may dry
Your hands (or they may not), but they
Spray germs into the air. If you wipe
Your hands on your pants just to be sure,
You may defeat the whole purpose
Of washing; your pants have germs
On them, too. The best way to dry
Your hands is to use a paper towel.

Most of these things I kind-of knew.
Two of them gave me moral support.
I've always hated those noisy blowers,
And never trusted them, either. Now,
I can avoid them with good conscience.
And I never realized other people wipe
Their hands on their pants, too: I thought
I was the only slob who did it. (And,
If you really want to know, we do it
Because we don't trust the blowers.)

We're living now in a time when
Washing (and drying) your hands well
Can actually save your life. So, I'm glad
I read the article, and I'll never
Use one of those blowers again.

Easter, 2020

This Easter was different.
We didn't have our usual houseful of guests.
(They all had to stay home.)

We didn't go to the sunrise service.
(It was cancelled). We drove to the shore
And saw the sun rise by ourselves.

We didn't go to a Sunday service.
(The churches were closed). We sat home
And watched a service on line.

We didn't eat at a fancy restaurant.
(The restaurants were closed.) We got take-out
Dinners from the local diner.

But the two of us did dress up, anyway,
And we sat down at our own festive table
And said our usual prayer of thanksgiving.
Our take-out meal wasn't as elaborate as
Our usual spread, but we enjoyed it.

And that, in the year of the virus,
Is how the two of us celebrated Easter.

FRIENDS

FRIENDS

We three old guys
Used to have long breakfasts
At Rick's, at least three mornings a week.
Now, like all the restaurants,
Rick's is closed.

We've tried, as couples,
To have cocktail parties on-line.
It's great to see them, but six people talking
On a screen (and often at once)
Can only get so far.

Out walking, we ran into
Brian, just back from Florida.
He and I had some catching up to do,
And we talked so long that my wife
Began walking away.

" I don't need friends,
Just as long as I have my wife."
That's what I used to say. And, yes,
She is the person I need the most,
But, no, I do need friends.

AL FRESCO

When you eat at Rick's,
You look out at the parking lot.
During the pandemic, you sit
Right in the parking lot.
Veronica has set up a few
Plastic tables on the asphalt
And roped the area off
With a bright yellow chain
To keep the traffic away.

It's a small parking lot but
Always very busy with cars
And trucks. There'll be three
Or four at the gas pumps
On the left, and five or six
Parked at the convenience
Store on the right. With all
The comings and goings, it
Takes some determination
To sit here and eat breakfast,
But we still do it, three days
A week. The change of venue
Doesn't bother us at all.

We do get annoyed, though,
When the eighteen-wheeler
That delivers the soft drinks
Parks in front of our table.
It totally blocks the view.

Two Old Friends

Two old guys are sitting on a bench
By the beach. They chat about
The news, as they do every week.
The beach is empty, except
For a mother and four children.
She keeps a wary eye, while
The children, wild with excitement,
Scamper here and there.

Each of the men loves this place,
This beach, this seaside town.
Each of them loves the other.
Tomorrow morning, one of them
Will be a thousand miles away,
And may never be able to return.
The other will be back here again,
Sitting on this same bench,
Sipping his morning coffee.

www.ingramcontent.com/pod-product-compliance
Lightning Source LLC
Chambersburg PA
CBHW032048040426
42449CB00007B/1025